DEDICATION

To the hundreds of young people whom I have
been privileged to teach, to know, and to
love, this book is respectfully dedicated.

E.R.M.

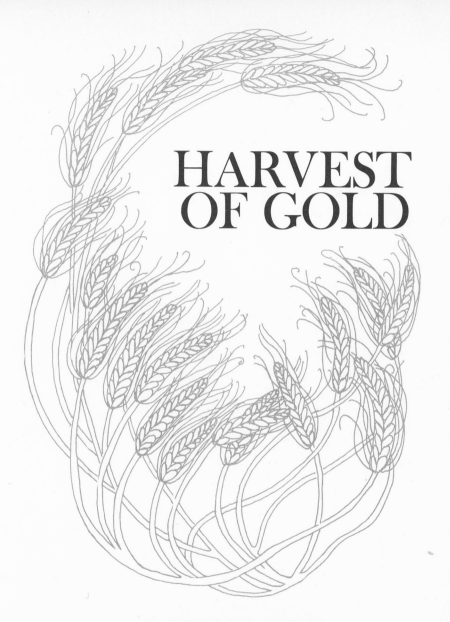

HARVEST
OF GOLD

By ERNEST R. MILLER

ILLUSTRATED BY DOROTHY PEEBLES

PUBLISHED BY THE C. R. GIBSON COMPANY

SPECIAL ACKNOWLEDGEMENT

Special thanks are due to Marian E. Miller
for encouragement, for aid in typing the
manuscript, and for assistance in obtaining
permission to use copyright materials; to the
Marquise de Chambrun for reading the
manuscript, for helpful suggestions, and for
the use of two of her poems; and to the Cincinnati Library for invaluable assistance in
finding necessary information.

Acknowledgments will be found on page 88.

CONTENTS

BEAUTY	9
MUSIC	17
LOVE	23
FRIENDSHIP	29
BROTHERHOOD	35
INSPIRATION	43
COURAGE	49
ACHIEVEMENT	55
TRUTH	59
HAPPINESS	67
FAITH	73
PATRIOTISM	81

INTRODUCTION

Much of the material for this anthology has been gleaned from a scrapbook containing bits of verse, maxims, and quotations which I have been collecting since early boyhood. These bits of treasure have been of inestimable worth to me through the years as a source of pleasure and inspiration as well as providing a greater appreciation of literature and beauty in all its forms. I have carried this scrapbook with me to distant lands, and in lonely hours found in it pleasure and as "light unto my feet."

From the days when I was a country boy with a weekly newspaper and an occasional magazine as my sole source of reading material to supplement the wonderful classics in the old McGuffey Readers, and through my years as a teacher, school administrator, and athletic coach on the high school, college, and university levels, my interests have undergone much change. This change is reflected in the materials in this anthology. Therefore the contents should be sufficiently varied as to provide something of interest and value to all.

Besides selections from the masters, there are a number of poems which have not before appeared in an anthology, and some which have not before been published. With full knowledge that I am not richly endowed with poetic genius, I have included a few of my own compositions. There need be no agitation on Parnassus.

It is hoped that in this anthology the reader will find pleasure, inspiration, and a greater meaning to life.

ERNEST R. MILLER

BEAUTY

What is lovely never dies,
But passes into other loveliness,
Star dust or sea-foam, flower, or wingéd air.

THOMAS BAILEY ALDRICH

To see a world in a Grain of Sand
    And a Heaven in a Wild Flower,
Hold infinity in the palm of your hand
    And Eternity in an hour!

WILLIAM BLAKE

When gilded head of crocus breaks the earth
    And blossoms tremble on the almond tree
The sun is warmer on my aging back
    And memories come crowding in to me.

The dragging winter months have lasted long
    And chill has kept me prisoned to my hearth
My senses dulled by many months disuse
    But suddenly it's spring again!

With eagerness I daily search them out:
    Remembered signs and joys returned —
The first dark hidden violet,
    The bursting gold of daffodil,
The early song of finch upon the bough,
    The scarlet flash of cardinal,
And I am young again
    Because
I find a sudden spring.

THE MARQUISE DE CHAMBRUN — SUDDEN SPRING

    Spring has come
Like the silver needle-note of a fife,
Like a white plume and a green lance
    and a glittering knife
And a jubilant drum.

JOSEPH AUSLANDER

Behind every flower stands God

JAPANESE PROVERB

I meant to do my work today
   But a brown bird sang in the apple tree,
And a butterfly flitted across the field,
   And all the leaves were calling me.

And the wind went sighing over the land,
   Tossing the grasses to and fro,
And a rainbow held out his shining hand —
   So what could I do but laugh and go?

RICHARD LE GALLIENNE — I MEANT TO DO MY WORK TODAY

Never lose an opportunity for seeing anything that is
beautiful; for beauty is God's handwriting — a wayside
sacrament. Welcome it in every fair face, in every fair sky,
in every fair flower, and thank God for it as a cup
of blessing.

RALPH WALDO EMERSON

My mind lets go a thousand things,
   Like dates of wars and deaths of kings,
And yet recalls the very hour —
   'Twas noon by yonder village tower,
And on the last blue noon of May —
   The wind came briskly up the way,
Crisping the brook beside the road;
   Then, passing here, set down its load
Of pine scents, and shook listlessly
   Two petals from that wild rose tree.

THOMAS BAILEY ALDRICH — MEMORY

There is something in the autumn that
        is native to my blood,
Touch of manner, hint of mood;
And my heart is like a rhyme,
With the yellow and the purple and the
        crimson keeping time.

The scarlet of the maples can shake me
        like a cry
Of bugles going by.
And my lonely spirit thrills
To see the frosty asters like smoke upon
        the hills.

There is something in October sets the
        gypsy blood astir;
We must rise and follow her,
When from every hill aflame,
She calls and calls each vagabond by name.

BLISS CARMAN — AN AUTUMN SONG

Whose woods these are I think I know.
    His house is in the village, though;
He will not see me stopping here
    To watch his woods fill up with snow.

My little horse must think it queer
    To stop without a farmhouse near
Between the woods and frozen lake
    The darkest evening of the year.

He gives his harness bells a little shake
    To ask if there is some mistake.
The only other sound's the sweep
    Of easy wind and downy flake.

The woods are lovely, dark and deep,
  But I have promises to keep,
And miles to go before I sleep,
  And miles to go before I sleep.

ROBERT FROST — STOPPING BY A WOODS
                ON A SNOWY EVENING

I shall keep some cool green memory in my heart
  To draw upon should days be bleak and cold.
I shall hold it like a cherished thing apart
  To turn to now or when I shall be old.
Perhaps a sweeping meadow, brightly green,
  Where grasses bend and the winds of heaven blow
Straight from the hand of God, as cool and clean
  As anything the heart of man can know.

Or it may be this green remembered tree
  That I shall turn to if the nights be long,
High on a hill, its cool boughs lifting free,
  And from its tip, a wild bird's joyous song.
A weary city dweller to survive
  Must keep some cool green memory alive.

GRACE NOLL CROWELL — KEEP SOME GREEN MEMORY ALIVE

A haze on the far horizon,
  The infinite, tender sky,
The ripe, rich tint of the cornfields,
  And the wild geese sailing high,—
And all over upland and lowland
  The charm of the goldenrod,—
Some of us call it Autumn,
  And others call it God.

W. H. CARRUTH

The miracles of nature do not seem miracles because they are so common. If no one had ever seen a flower, even a dandelion would be the most startling event in the world.

ANONYMOUS

Life has loveliness to sell—
    All beautiful and splendid things,
Blue waves whitened on a cliff,
    Soaring fire that sways and sings,
And children's faces looking up
    Holding wonder like a cup.

Life has loveliness to sell—
    Scent of pine trees in the rain,
Music like a curve of gold,
    Eyes that love you, arms that hold,
And for the spirit's safe delight,
    Holy thoughts that star the night.

Spend all that you have for loveliness,
    Buy it and never count the cost;
For one white singing hour of peace
    Count many a year of strife well lost,
And for a breath of ecstasy
    Give all that you have been, or could be.

SARA TEASDALE — BARTER

I took the day to search for God,
    And found Him not. But as I trod
By rocky ledge, through woods untamed,
    Just where one scarlet lily flamed,
I saw His footprints in the sod.

BLISS CARMAN

When I would be content and increase confidence in the
power and wisdom of Almighty God, I will walk the meadows
by some stream, and there contemplate the lilies that take no
care, and those very many other little living creatures that
are not only created, but fed, (man knows not how) by the
God of Nature, and therefore trust in Him.

IZAAK WALTON

I who have seen the stars at midnight,
    The clean cut flight of birds,
Know with a swift assurance
    The idleness of words.
It is as though quaint nets were spread
    To catch the flying snow,
Or wooden buckets set to save
    The silver starlight glow.

RACHEL BRODY

If on this night of still, white cold,
    I can remember May,
New green of trees and underbrush,
A hillside orchard's mounting flush,
The scent of earth and noon's blue hush,
    A robin's jaunty way.

If on this night of bitter frost,
    I know such things can be,
That lovely May is true — ah, well,
I shall believe the tales men tell,
Wonders of bliss and asphodel
    And immortality.

HORTENSE FLEXNER — IMMORTALITY

Strange that the spring has come
   On meadow and vale and hill
For here in the sunless slum
   My bosom is frozen still.
And I wear the wadded things
   Of the dreary winter days,
But out of the heart of this little flower
   God gazes into my face.

TOYOHIKO KAGAWA

All things bright and beautiful,
   All creatures great and small,
All things wise and wonderful,
   The Lord God made them all.

CECIL FRANCES ALEXANDER

Look at Nature. She never wearies of saying over her floral
pater noster. In the crevices of Cyclopian walls, on the mounds
that bury huge cities, in the dust where men lie, dust also — still
that same sweet prayer and benediction. The amen of Nature
is always a flower.

OLIVER WENDELL HOLMES

MUSIC

Music is the harmonious voice of creation;
an echo of the invisible world; one note
of the divine concord which the entire
universe is destined one day to sound.

GIUSEPPE MAZZINI

Music's the cordial of a troubled breast
The softest remedy that grief can find;
The gentle spell that charms our care to rest
And calms the ruffled passions of the mind.
   Music does all our joys refine,
   And gives the relish to our wine.

JOHN OLDHAM

Music, the universal language of mankind, is also a form of beauty at its best. As language differs among peoples, so does the language of music differ with time, place, background and experience; but if it is true music, it strikes a responsive chord.

In a Japanese home at Christmas-time, I was the only person in the group who spoke English. Yet ways of communication were found. Thinking of home, I hummed softly to myself, "Silent Night." To my surprise, the French guest, the German guest and the Japanese family joined in singing the universally inspiring Christmas song, each in his own language, yet in the same language, the language of the heart.

ERNEST R. MILLER

How many of us ever stop to think
   Of music as a wondrous magic link
With God; taking sometimes the place of prayer,
   When words have failed us 'neath the weight of care?
Music, that knows no country, race or creed;
   But gives to each according to his need.

ANONYMOUS

Music has been called the speech of the angels; I will go farther and call it the speech of God Himself.

CHARLES KINGSLEY

18

Many love music but for music's sake,
Many because her touches can awake
Thoughts that repose within the breast
    half-dead,
And rise to follow where she loves to lead.
What various feelings come from days
    gone by!
What tears from far-off sources dim the eye!
Few, when light fingers with sweet voices
    play,
And melodies swell, pause, and melt away,
Mind how at every touch, at every tone,
A spark of life hath glistened and hath gone.

WALTER SAVAGE LANDOR — MANY LOVE MUSIC

When music sounds, gone is the earth I know,
    And all her lovelier things even lovelier grow;
Her flowers in vision flame, her forest trees
    Lift burdened branches, stilled with ecstasies.

When music sounds, out of the water rise
    Naiads whose beauty dims my waking eyes,
Rapt in strange dream burns each enchanted face,
    With solemn echoing stirs their dwelling-place.

When music sounds, all that I was I am
    Ere to this haunt of brooding dust I came;
And from Time's woods break into distant song
    The swift-winged hours, as I hasten along.

WALTER DE LA MARE — MUSIC

Where words fail, music speaks.

HANS CHRISTIAN ANDERSEN

You ask me where I get my ideas. That I cannot tell you with
certainty. They come unsummoned, directly, indirectly —
I could seize them with my hands — out in the open air, in
the woods, while walking, in the silence of the nights, at dawn,
excited by moods which are translated by the poet into words,
by me into tones that sound and roar and storm about me
till I have set them down in notes.

LUDWIG VAN BEETHOVEN

Music is in all growing things;
And underneath the silky wings
   Of smallest insects there is stirred
   A pulse of air that must be heard;
Earth's silence lives, and throbs, and sings.

GEORGE PARSONS LATHROP

We love music for the buried hopes, the garnered memories,
the tender feelings it can summon at a touch.

SAMUEL ROGERS

And music, too — dear music! that can touch
   Beyond all else the soul that loves it much —
Now heard far off, so far as but to seem
   Like the faint, exquisite music of a dream.

THOMAS MOORE

The meaning of song goes deep. Who in logical words can
explain the effect music has on us? A kind of inarticulate,
unfathomable speech, which leads us to the edge of the infinite,
and lets us for a moment gaze into that!

THOMAS CARLYLE

There is in souls a sympathy with sounds;
    And as the mind is pitch'd, the ear is pleased
With melting airs or martial, brisk, or grave;
    Some chord in unison with what we hear
Is touch'd within us, and the heart replies.

WILLIAM COWPER

There's music in the sighing of a reed;
    There's music in the gushing of a rill;
There's music in all things, if we have ears;
    The earth is but the music of the spheres.

GEORGE GORDON, LORD BYRON

How sweet the moonlight sleeps upon this bank!
Here we will sit, and let the sounds of music
Creep in our ears; soft stillness and the night
Become the touches of sweet harmony.
Sit, Jessica: look, how the floor of heaven
Is thick inlaid with patines of bright gold;
There's not the smallest orb which thou behold'st
But in his motion like an angel sings,
Still quiring to the young-eyed cherubins.
Such harmony is in immortal souls;
But whilst this muddy vesture of decay
Doth grossly close it in, we cannot hear it.

WILLIAM SHAKESPEARE

Music was a thing of the soul — a roselipped shell that
murmured of the eternal sea — a strange bird singing the
songs of another shore.

JOSIAH GILBERT HOLLAND

The soul of music slumbers in the shell
    Till waked and kindled by the master's spell;
And feeling hearts, touch them but rightly, pour
    A thousand melodies unheard of before.

E. E. LANDON

Music is a revelation; a revelation loftier
than all wisdom and all philosophy.

LUDWIG VON BEETHOVEN

Music is Love in search of a word.

AMBROSE BIERCE

When I hear music I fear no danger, I am invulnerable, I see
no foe. I am related to the earliest times, and to the latest.

HENRY DAVID THOREAU

In holy music's golden speech
    Remotest notes to notes respond:
Each octave is a world; yet each
    Vibrates to worlds beyond its own.

AUBREY THOMAS DE VERE

LOVE

By the accident of fortune a man may rule
the world for a time, but by virtue of love he may
rule the world forever.

LAO-TSE

Love is the only bow on life's dark cloud. It is the Morning
and the Evening Star. It shines upon the cradle of the babe, and
sheds its radiance upon the quiet tomb. It is the Mother of Art,
inspirer of poet, patriot, and philosopher. It is the air and light
of every heart, builder of every home, kindler of every fire on
every hearth. It was the first dream of immortality. It fills
the world with melody, for music is the voice of Love. Love is
the magician, the enchanter, that changes worthless things to
joy, and makes right royal kings of common clay. It is the
perfume of the wondrous flower — the heart — and without
that sacred passion, . . . we are less than beasts; but with it,
earth and heaven are gods.

ROBERT G. INGERSOLL

Love is something eternal — the aspects may change, but not
the essence. There is the same difference in a person before and
after he is in love as there is in an unlighted lamp and one that
is burning. The lamp was there and it is a good lamp, but now
it is shedding light, too, and that is its real function.

VINCENT VAN GOGH

There is nothing holier in this life of ours that the first
consciousness of love — the first fluttering of its silken wings —
the first rising sound and breath of that wind which is soon
to sweep through the soul, to purify or destroy.

HENRY WADSWORTH LONGFELLOW

The greatest happiness in the world is the conviction that
we are loved, loved for ourselves, or rather loved in spite
of ourselves.

VICTOR HUGO

Love is the enchanted dawn of every heart.

ALPHONSE DE LAMARTINE

Love is the master key that opens the gates of happiness.

OLIVER WENDELL HOLMES

All the breath and the bloom of the year
in the bag of one bee;
   All the wonder and wealth of the mine
in the heart of one gem;
In the core of one pearl all the shade and
the shine of the sea;
   Breath and bloom, shade and shine, —
wonder, wealth, and — how far above them —
   Truth, that's brighter than gem,
   Truth, that's purer than pearl, —
Brightest truth, purest trust in the universe —
all were for me
   In the kiss of one girl.

ROBERT BROWNING — SUMMUM BONUM

It is strange to talk of miracles, revelations, inspiration,
and the like, as things past, while love remains.

HENRY DAVID THOREAU

This is the miracle that happens every time to those who really
love: the more they give, the more they possess of that precious
nourishing love from which flowers and children have their
strength and which could help all human beings if they would
take it without doubting.

RAINER MARIA RILKE

Into my heart's treasury
    I slipped a coin
That Time cannot take
    Nor a thief purloin —
O better than the minting
    Of a gold-crowned king
Is the safe-kept memory
    Of a lovely thing.

SARA TEASDALE — THE COIN

With thee all tales are sweet; each clime
has charms; earth — sea alike — our world
within our arms.

GEORGE GORDON, LORD BYRON

                    . . . Love is not love
Which alters when it alteration finds,
Or bends with the remover to remove.

WILLIAM SHAKESPEARE

Love is a second life; it grows into the soul,
warms every vein, and beats in every pulse.

JOSEPH ADDISON

That is the true season of love, when we believe that we alone
can love, that no one could ever have loved so before us, and
that no one will love in the same way as us.

JOHANN WOLFGANG VON GOETHE

It is a beautiful necessity of our nature to love something.

DOUGLAS JERROLD

Since we parted yester eve,
  I do love thee, love, believe,
Twelve times dearer, twelve hours longer,—
  One dream deeper, one night stronger,
One sun surer, — thus much more
  Than I loved thee, love, before.

EDWARD ROBERT BULWER-LYTTON — SINCE WE PARTED

Love is a madness most discreet.

WILLIAM SHAKESPEARE

I know a road that leads into a city,
Also a lane that finds a cooling stream,
Where ferns may look down at their
            green reflection
And sway with the winds and dream —
            and dream.

I know a path that leads into a forest,
Lined with purple shadows of the night,
While poplars bend somewhere along a
            hilltop
Ringing their silver bells in quick
            delight.

I know a trail that dances over hill-tops
Reaching high for clouds that sail the
            blue,
But best I know a path that leads me
            homeward —
A lane that takes me home to friends —
            and you.

ERNEST R. MILLER — A LANE THAT LEADS TO HOME

So long as we love, we serve. So long as we are loved by others I would almost say we are indispensable; and no man is useless while he has a friend.

ROBERT LOUIS STEVENSON

I love her with a love as still
As a broad river's peaceful might,
Which by high tower and lowly mill,
Goes wandering at its own will,
And yet does ever flow aright.

JAMES RUSSELL LOWELL

When, in disgrace with fortune and men's eyes,
I all alone beweep my outcast state,
And trouble deaf heaven with my bootless cries,
And look upon myself, and curse my fate,
Wishing me like to one more rich in hope,
Featured like him, like him with friends possess'd,
Desiring this man's art and that man's scope,
With what I most enjoy contented least;
Yet in these thoughts myself almost despising,
Haply I think on thee, and then my state,
Like to the lark at break of day arising
From sullen earth, sings hymns at heaven's gate;
    For thy sweet love remember'd such wealth
        brings
    That then I scorn to change my state with kings.

WILLIAM SHAKESPEARE, SONNET XXIX

To Adam, Paradise was home. To the good among his descendants, home is paradise.

JULIUS C. HARE

FRIENDSHIP

Every house where love abides
 And friendship is a guest,
Is surely home, and home, sweet home
 For there the heart can rest.

HENRY VAN DYKE

I am united with my friend in heart,
What matters if our place is wide apart?

ANONYMOUS

These are the things I prize
    And hold of dearest worth:
Light of the sapphire skies,
Peace of the silent hills,
Shelter of the forests, comfort of the grass,
Music of the birds, murmur of the little rills,
Shadows of cloud that swiftly pass,
    And after showers,
    The smell of flowers
And of the good brown earth —
And best of all, along the way, friendship
    and mirth.

HENRY VAN DYKE — THESE THINGS I PRIZE

A friend is a person with whom I may be sincere. Before
him I may think aloud.

RALPH WALDO EMERSON

There are veins in the hills where jewels hide
    And gold lies buried deep;
There are harbor-towns where the great ships ride,
    And fame and fortune sleep;
But land and sea though we tireless rove,
And follow each trail to the end,
    Whatever the wealth of our treasure-trove,
The best we shall find is a friend.

JOHN J. MOMENT — THE BEST TREASURE

A friend is a priceless gem for the crown of life here
and a cherished star in memory forever.

CYRUS S. NUSBAUM

My friends are little lamps to me,
   Their radiance warms and cheers my ways,
And all the pathway dark and lone
   Is brightened by their rays.

I try to keep them bright by faith,
   And never let them dim with doubt;
For every time I lose a friend
   A little lamp goes out.

ELIZABETH WHITTEMORE — MY FRIENDS

He that wrongs a friend
Wrongs himself more, and ever bears
   about
A silent court of justice in his breast,
Himself the judge and jury, and himself
The prisoner at the bar ever condemned.

ALFRED, LORD TENNYSON

I would empty thy chalice of heart-ache and pain,
   Would freshen the desert with flowers and rain,
Would draw out the bitter and pour in the sweet,
   And remove every thorn from the way of thy feet;
Would sing in the gladness of summer and bloom,
   And sing out the sadness of winter and gloom,
Would lessen the load by enlarging thy life,
   I would sing back repose, and would sing away strife.

CHARLES C. WOODS — FRIEND

Oh, the comfort, the inexpressible comfort of feeling safe with a person; having neither to weigh thoughts nor measure words, but to pour them all out, just as they are, chaff and grain together, knowing that a faithful hand will take and sift them, keep what is worth keeping, and then, with the breath of kindness, blow the rest away.

DINAH MARIA MULOCK CRAIK

Silences make the real conversations between friends. Not the saying but the never needing to say is what counts.

MARGARET LEE RUNBECK

Let me live in my house by the side of
    the road
Where the race of men go by;
They are good, they are bad, they are
    weak, they are strong,
Wise, foolish — so am I.
Then why should I sit in the scorner's
    seat,
Or hurl the cynic's ban?
Let me live in my house by the side of
    the road
And be a friend of man.

SAM WALTER FOSS

In the hours of distress and misery, the eyes of every mortal turn to friendship; in the hours of gladness and conviviality, what is our want? It is friendship. When the heart overflows with gratitude, or with any other sweet or sacred sentiment, what is the word to which it would give utterance? A friend.

WALTER SAVAGE LANDOR

Because of a friend, life is a little stronger, fuller, more gracious thing for the friend's existence, whether he be near or far. If the friend is close at hand, that is best; but if he is far away he still is there to think of, to wonder about, to hear from, to write to, to share life and experience with, to serve, to honor, to admire, to love.

ARTHUR C. BENSON

Beautiful and rich is an old friendship,
    Grateful to the touch as ancient ivory,
Smooth as aged wine, or sheen tapestry
    Where light has lingered, intimate and long.
Full of tears and warm is an old friendship
    That asks no longer deeds of gallantry,
Or any deed at all — save that the friend
        shall be
Alive and breathing somewhere like a song.

EUNICE TIETJENS — OLD FRIENDSHIP

There is no friend like the old friend who has shared
        our morning days,
No greeting like his welcome, no homage like his praise;
Fame is the scentless sunflower, with gaudy crown of
        gold;
But friendship is the breathing rose, with sweets in
        every fold.

OLIVER WENDELL HOLMES

What is it to stay young? It is the ability to hold fast to old friends and to make new ones, to open our hearts quickly to a light knock on the door.

ANONYMOUS

I like not only to be loved, but also to be told that I am loved.
I am not sure that you are of the same kind. But the realm of
silence is large enough beyond the grave. This is the world
of light and speech, and I shall take leave to tell you that you
are very dear.

GEORGE ELIOT

Crossing the uplands of time,
    Skirting the borders of night,
Scaling the face of the peak of dreams,
    We enter the region of light,
And hastening on with eager intent,
    Arrive at the rainbow's end,
And here uncover the pot of gold
    Buried deep in the heart of a friend.

GRACE GOODHUE COOLIDGE — A FRIEND

I ask but one thing of you, only one,
    That always you will be my dream of you;
    That never shall I wake to find untrue
All this I have believed and rested on,
Forever vanished, like a vision gone
    Out into the night. Alas, how few
    There are who strike in us a chord we knew
Existed, but so seldom heard its tone
    We tremble at the half-forgotten sound.
The world is full of rude awakenings
    And heaven-born castles shattered to the ground,
Yet still our human longing vainly clings
    To a belief in beauty through all wrongs.
    O stay your hand, and leave my heart its songs!

AMY LOWELL — TO A FRIEND

BROTHERHOOD

No man is an island, entire of itself;
every man is a piece of the continent,
a part of the main.

JOHN DONNE

Try to care about something in this vast world besides the gratification of small selfish desires. Try to care for what is best in thought and action — something that is good apart from the accidents of your own lot. Look on other lives besides your own. See what their troubles are, and how they are borne.

GEORGE ELIOT

Shortly after my taking over as Principal of the American School, Kyoto, Japan, during the Occupation, one of our kindergarten teachers came to my office to inform me that the eight-year-old son of one of the Japanese kindergarten assistants had died the previous night. I suggested that the five American kindergarten teachers and I call at the bereaved home to pay our respects. On the way we purchased flowers and fruit, a Japanese custom, as evidence of our concern and respect. When we arrived at the home, the mother was away making funeral arrangements, but the child's grandmother, on her knees, opened the sliding door, and, bowing low, invited us in.

After removing our shoes, we entered and were seated on the tatami. Typical of Orientals, the grandmother was determined not to show her grief, but the surprise visit by people who were so recently at war with her country broke through her stoic resolve and she could not conceal the tears which dimmed her eyes.

After the grandmother had placed our flowers and fruit on a small silk-covered table or altar, one of the teachers realized that our hostess wished me to kneel in prayer at this altar. The young teachers immediately suggested that they join me. So a Buddhist grandmother and six Americans, I (a Presbyterian), a Baptist, two Catholics, a Jew, and a Lutheran knelt in prayer in this home where sorrow had laid its heavy hand. I could not but wonder whose voice was heard — each I thought, and then I wished that the whole world might look in on this scene where the death of a child had brought together in a common bond people diverse in customs, language, race, and creed, and where the consuming hatred of the recent war had melted away under the light of human sympathy, understanding, and love. Prejudice, however deeply ingrained, would, I thought, fall away like a shabby garment and "peace and good will to men" would come nearer to realization. "A little child shall lead them," I remembered.

To us Americans our mission was but a normal response when sorrow lays its heavy load, and our reward was the inner satisfaction of having done what decent people ought to do. However, word of our visit spread among the forty Japanese employed at our school and widely through the Japanese community at large. The harvest of goodwill, manifested in uncounted ways, that came to us and to Americans generally was an unhoped-for reward.

When Mitsuko-san returned to school she came to my office. As she attempted to thank me for our thoughtfulness, in spite of her resolve, tears cascaded down her face and she could but put her head on my shoulder and weep, as mothers everywhere must do when death takes one of their own. When she had recovered somewhat, she placed in my tie a beautiful pearl, perhaps her only jewel, as an expression of gratitude, but also, I thought, as an appropriate symbol of the love and mutual respect that were developing between the Japanese and American people. And so I hold this "pearl of great price" as a cherished memento of an experience, born in sorrow, yet rich in love, in which the death of a child cemented the bonds of friendship and love between two peoples and reaffirmed the essential kinship of the whole human race.

ERNEST R. MILLER — THE DEATH OF A CHILD

Count Leo Tolstoy, author of *War and Peace*, set forth his interpretation of the Golden Rule in his *Confessions of Faith:*

> I believe that the will of God is that every man should love his fellowman, and should act toward others as he desires that they should act toward him.

> I believe that the reason of life is for each of us simply to grow in love.

> I believe that the growth in love will contribute more than any force to establish the Kingdom of God on earth —

> To replace a social life in which division, falsehood, violence, are all powerful, with a new order in which humanity, truth, and brotherhood will reign.

In men whom men condemn as ill,
    I find so much of goodness still;
In men whom men pronounce divine,
    I find so much of sin and blot,
I hesitate to draw a line
    Between the two where God has not.

JOAQUIN MILLER

God, what a world, if men in street and mart
    Felt that same kinship of the human heart
Which makes them, in the face of fire and flood,
    Rise to the meaning of true brotherhood.

ELLA WHEELER WILCOX

No man has come to true greatness who has not felt that his life belongs to his race, and that which God gives him, He gives him for mankind.

PHILLIPS BROOKS

38

Brief, so brief — the words were falling
   Ere men had time to note and weigh;
As if the gods were calling
   From some Homeric yesterday.

No impulse this, no actor speaking
   Of thoughts which come by happy chance;
The man, the place, were God's own seeking;
   The words are our inheritance.

A pause, a hush, a wonder growing;
   A prophet's vision understood;
In that strange spell of his bestowing,
   They dreamed, with him, of Brotherhood.

HARRISON D. MASON — ABRAHAM LINCOLN AT GETTYSBURG

Someone wrote of Lincoln, "He makes all mankind just a bit taller."

ANONYMOUS

His life was so gentle, and the elements
So mix'd in him, that Nature might stand up
And say to all the world, "This was a man!"

WILLIAM SHAKESPEARE

We are all citizens of one world, we are all of one blood. To hate a man because he was born in another country, because he speaks a different language, or because he takes a different view on this subject or that, is a great folly. Desist, I implore you, for we are all equally human . . . Let us have but one end in view, the welfare of humanity.

JOHANN AMOS COMENIUS

At length there dawns the glorious day
  By prophets long foretold;
At length the chorus clearer grows
  That shepherds heard of old.
The day of growing Brotherhood
  Breaks on our eager eyes,
And human hatreds flee before
  The radiant Eastern skies.

For what are the sundering strains of blood,
  Or caste or ancient creed?
One claim unites all men of God
  To serve each human need . . .

One common faith unites us all,
  We seek one common goal,
One tender comfort broods upon
  The struggling human soul.

To this clear call of Brotherhood
  Our hearts responsive ring;
We join the modern new crusade
  Of our great Lord and King.

OZORA STEARNS DAVIS — BROTHERHOOD

It is not enough that you should understand about applied
science in order that your work may increase man's blessings.
Concern for man himself and his fate must always form the
chief interest of all technical endeavors, concern for the great
unsolved problems of the organization of labor and the
distribution of goods — in order that the creations of our
mind shall be a blessing and not a curse to mankind. Never
forget this in the midst of your diagrams and equations.

ALBERT EINSTEIN

For me — to have made one soul
    The better for my birth;
To have added one flower
    To the garden of the earth;

To have struck one blow for truth
    In the daily fight with lies;
To have done one deed of right
    In the face of calumnies;

To have sown in the souls of men
    One thought that will not die —
To have been a link in the chain of life
    Shall be immortality.

EDWIN HATCH — TOWARDS FIELDS OF LIGHT

We have committed the Golden Rule to memory;
let us now commit it to life.

EDWIN MARKHAM

You go to your church and I'll go to mine,
    But let's walk along together;
Our Father built them side by side,
    So let's walk along together.

PHILLIPS H. LORD

With malice toward none, with charity for all, with firmness
in the right as God gives us to see the right, let us strive on to
finish the work we are in, to bind up the nation's wounds, . . .
to do all which may achieve and cherish a just and lasting
peace among ourselves and with all nations.

ABRAHAM LINCOLN

I expect to pass this way but once; any good therefore that I can do, or any kindness that I can show to any fellow creature, let me do it now. Let me not defer or neglect it, for I shall not pass this way again.

ETIENNE DE GRELLET

Teach me to feel another's woe,
  To hide the faults I see,
That mercy I to others show
  That mercy show to me.

ALEXANDER POPE

Just do what you can. It's not enough merely to exist. It's not enough to say, "I'm earning enough to live and support my family. I do my work well. I'm a good father. I'm a good husband." That's all very well. *But you must do something more.* Seek always to do some good, somewhere. Every man has to seek in his own way to make his own self more noble and to realize his own true worth. You must give some time to your fellowman. Even if it's a little thing, do something for those who have need of help, something for which you get no pay but the privilege of doing it. For remember, you don't live in a world all your own. *Your brothers are here, too.*

DR. ALBERT SCHWEITZER

INSPIRATION

Every great and commanding moment in the annals
of the world is the triumph of some enthusiasm.

RALPH WALDO EMERSON

Persistence. The temptation to be discouraged is common to every man. Walt Disney was dismissed from a major newspaper and told that he had no talent as an artist; Richard Byrd, famous pilot, and who was first to reach the South Pole, crash-landed the first two times he soloed in a plane, and the third time he flew head on into another plane; Rod Serling wrote and marketed 40 stories before he sold one; Zane Grey was fired by five newspapers because he couldn't do the job as a reporter.

ANONYMOUS

Some men see things as they are and say, why? I dream of things that never were and say, why not?

GEORGE BERNARD SHAW

Far away there in the sunshine are my highest aspirations. I may not reach them, but I can look up and see their beauty, believe in them, and try to follow them.

LOUISA MAY ALCOTT

My old self
    Whispers from behind me:
"There is danger ahead!"
    My young self cries:
"On! On!"

AKIKO YOSANO

It seems to me that we can never give up longing and wishing while we are thoroughly alive. There are certain things we feel to be beautiful and good, and we must hunger after them.

GEORGE ELIOT

It is not the critic who counts; not the man who points out how the strong man stumbled, or where the doer of deeds could have done them better. The credit belongs to the man who is actually in the arena, whose face is marred by dust and sweat and blood; who strives valiantly; who errs and comes short again and again; who knows the great enthusiasms, the great devotions; who spends himself in a worthy cause; who at best, knows in the end the triumph of high achievement, and who, at the worst, if he fails, at least fails while daring greatly, so that his place shall never be with those timid souls who knew neither victory nor defeat.

THEODORE ROOSEVELT

Man's mind stretched to a new idea never goes back to its original dimensions.

OLIVER WENDELL HOLMES

It takes a lot of patience and God
    To build a life,
It takes a lot of courage
    To meet the stress and strife;
It takes a lot of loving
    To make the wrong come right;
It takes a lot of patience and God
    To build a life

ANONYMOUS

I am tired of hearing of self-made men. There is not a self-made man in the world. The so-called self-made man is the man who seized his opportunities and those given to him by circumstance and has made use of them.

LUCIUS TUTTLE

The poorest of all men is not the man without a cent; it is the man without a dream.

If you have built castles in the air, your work need not be lost; that is where they should be. Now put foundations under them.

HENRY DAVID THOREAU

When I was young I was amazed at Plutarch's statement that the elder Cato began at the age of eighty to learn Greek. I am amazed no longer. Old age is ready to undertake tasks youth shirked because they would take too long.

W. SOMERSET MAUGHAM

Tomorrow — oh, it will never be
    If we should live a thousand years!
Our time is all today, today,
    The same, though changed; and
        while it flies
With still small voice the moments say:
    "Today, today, be wise, be wise."

JAMES MONTGOMERY — TODAY

Genius, that power which dazzles mortal eyes,
Is often perseverance in disguise.

HENRY WILLARD AUSTIN

To be seventy years young is sometimes far more cheerful and hopeful than to be forty years old.

OLIVER WENDELL HOLMES

It is not for man to rest in absolute contentment. He is born
to hopes and aspirations as sparks fly upward unless he has
brutified his nature and quenched the spirit of immortality
which is his portion.

ROBERT SOUTHEY

Do not pray for easy lives; pray to be stronger men! Do not
pray for tasks equal to your powers, pray for powers equal
to your tasks. Then the doing of your work shall be no miracle,
but you shall be a miracle. Every day you shall wonder at
yourself, at the richness of life which has come to you by the
grace of God.

PHILLIPS BROOKS

Inspiration is a fragile thing . . . just a breeze, touching the
green foliage of a city park, just a whisper from the soul of a
friend. Just a line of verse clipped from some forgotten
magazine . . . or a paragraph standing out from the chapters
of a book.
Inspiration . . . who can say where it is born, and why it leaves
us? Who can tell the reasons for its being or not being?
Only this . . . I think inspiration comes from the Heart of
Heaven to give the lift of wings, and the breath of divine
music to those of us who are earthbound.

MARGARET SANGSTER

He who has conquered doubt and fear has conquered failure.
Doubt has killed more splendid projects, shattered more
ambitious schemes, strangled more effective geniuses, neutralized
more superb efforts, blasted more fine intellects, thwarted more
splendid ambitions than any other enemy of the race.

JAMES ALLEN

The most powerful weapon on earth is the human soul on fire.

MARSHAL FERDINAND FOCH

The journey of a thousand miles begins with one step.

LAO-TSE

God be praised,
Antonio Stradivari had an eye
That winces at false work and loves
   the true . . .
And for my fame — when any master holds
'Twixt chin and hand a violin of mine,
He will be glad that Stradivari lived,
Made violins, and made of the best . . .

I say not God Himself can make man's best
Without best men to help Him . . .
   'Tis God gives skill,
But not without men's hands: He could not make
Antonio Stradivari's violins
Without Antonio.

GEORGE ELIOT: STRADIVARIUS

COURAGE

He either fears his fate too much,
   Or his deserts are small,
That puts it not unto the touch
   To win or lose it all.

JAMES GRAHAM, MARQUIS OF MONTROSE

Keep thou thy dreams — the tissue of all wings
    Is woven first from them; from dreams are made
The precious and imperishable things,
    Whose loveliness lives on, and does not fade.

VIRNA SHEARD

To suffer woes which Hope thinks infinite;
To forgive wrongs darker than death or
      night;
    To defy Power, which seems
      omnipotent;
    To love and bear; to hope till Hope
      creates
From its own wreck the thing it contem-
      plates;
    Neither to change, nor falter, nor
      repent:
This, like thy glory, Titan, is to be
Good, great and joyous, beautiful and
      free;
This is alone Life, Joy, Empire, and
      Victory.

PERCY BYSSHE SHELLEY

Sweet are the uses of adversity;
Which, like the toad, ugly and venomous,
Wears yet a precious jewel in his head;
And this our life, exempt from public haunt,
Finds tongues in trees, books in the running
    brooks,
Sermons in stones, and good in everything.

WILLIAM SHAKESPEARE

Let me pray not to be sheltered from dangers but to be fearless in facing them.

Let me not beg for the stilling of my pain, but for the heart to conquer it.

Let me not look for allies in life's battlefield, but to my own strength.

Let me crave not in anxious fear to be saved, but hope for the patience to win my freedom.

Grant me that I may not be a coward, feeling your mercy in my success alone; but let me find the grasp of your hand in failure.

RABINDRANATH TAGORE — PRAYER FOR COURAGE

So I never quite despair,
   Nor let my courage fail;
And some day when skies are fair,
   Up the bay my ships will sail.

ROBERT BARRY COFFIN

Courage, the highest gift, that scorns to bend
   To mean devices for a sordid end,
Courage — an independent spark from Heaven's bright throne,
   By which the soul stands raised, triumphant, high, alone.
Courage, the mighty attribute of power above,
   By which those great in war are great in love.
The spring of all brave acts are seated here,
   As falsehoods draw their sordid birth from fear.

GEORGE FARQUHAR — COURAGE

He who loses wealth loses much; he who loses a friend loses more; but he that loses his courage loses all.

MIGUEL DE CERVANTES

Courage is the price life exacts for granting peace.
The soul that knows it not, knows no release
  From little things;

Knows not the livid loneliness of fear
Nor mountain heights, where bitter joy can hear
  The sound of wings.

How can life grant us boon of living, compensate
For dull gray ugliness and pregnant hate
  Unless we dare

The soul's dominion? Each time we make a choice, we pay
With courage to behold resistless day
  And count it fair.

AMELIA EARHART — COURAGE

In the hills of life there are two trails. One lies along the higher
sunlit fields — where those who travel see afar, and the light
lingers long after the sun is down. And one lies along the lower
ground — where those who journey look over their shoulders
with eyes of dread, and gloomy shadows gather long before
the day is done.

HAROLD BELL WRIGHT

I have lived eighty-six years. I have watched men climb to
success, hundreds of them, and of all the elements that are
important for success, the most important is faith. No great
thing comes to any man unless he has courage.

JAMES CARDINAL GIBBONS

Physical strength is measured by what we can carry; spiritual
by what we can bear.

Low I kneel through the night again,
    Hear my prayer, if my prayer be right!
Take for Thy token my proud heart broken.
    God, guide my arm! I go back to the fight.

ANONYMOUS

Courage is armor
    A blind man wears;
The calloused scar
    Of outlived repairs;
Courage is Fear
    That has said its prayers.

KARLE W. BAKER

Do not wish for self-confidence in yourself; get it from within.
Nobody can give it to you. It is one of the greatest assets of
life. Self-confidence comes to you every time you are knocked
down and get up. A little boy was asked how he learned to
skate: "Oh, by getting up every time I fell down," he replied . . .
Self-trust is the first secret of success.

RALPH WALDO EMERSON

I do not ask to walk smooth paths
    Nor bear an easy load.
I pray for strength and fortitude
    To climb the rock-strewn road.

Give me such courage I can scale
    The hardest peaks alone,
And transform every stumbling block
    Into a steppingstone.

GAIL BROOK BURKETT — PRAYER

You asked me, "What is courage?" And I took
   The dictionary down and spelled it out.
For such a little boy, the heavy book
   Was ponderous. You twisted it about;
You said, "It's being brave — and what is that?"
   You said, "It's not fear — am I afraid?"
"Does courage arch its back up like a cat,
   And spit at everything it meets?" you said.

Perplexed, we closed the book and took a walk,
   And came where fire had worked untimely death;
The woods were gone. But on a slender stalk
   A flower inched for life. I caught my breath.
"Courage," I said, and took you by the hand,
"Is one white flower in a fire-swept land."

HELEN FRAZEE-BOWER — COURAGE

Keep your fears to yourself, but share your courage with others.

PHILLIPS BROOKS

Do you fear the force of the wind,
   The slash of the rain?
Go face them and fight them,
   Be savage again.
Go hungry and cold like the wolf,
   Go wade like the crane:
The palms of your hands will thicken,
   The skin of your cheek will tan,
You'll grow ragged and weary and swarthy,
   But you'll walk like a man!

HAMLIN GARLAND — DO YOU FEAR THE WIND?

ACHIEVEMENT

Let us, then, be up and doing,
With a heart for any fate;
Still achieving, still pursuing,
Learn to labor and to wait.

HENRY WADSWORTH LONGFELLOW — ACHIEVEMENT

The spirit of "Let George do it" will never win in sports
or in the game of life.

FIELDING H. YOST

Football is a game in which millions of Americans take part,
and yet is completely uninhibited by racial barriers. This has
always been true on the field, and God willing, it will be true
off the field in a very short time. It is a game of action where
the only success the individual has is to be a part of the
successful whole. It is a game that gives 100 per cent elation
when you win and demands 100 per cent determination and
resolution when you lose. Like the game of life, it teaches that
work and perseverance and competitive drive and respect for
authority is the price all must pay to achieve any goal that is
worthwhile.
Most athletes possess a leadership ability, but, unfortunately,
leadership rests not only on ability but also on commitment
and loyalty and pride. Heart power is the strength of America,
and hate power is the weakness of the world. Mental toughness
is the perfectly disciplined will and it must be the will of the
man who leads. The will is character in action. If we would
create something, we must be something.

VINCE LOMBARDI

Athletic sports are the great levelers, the great equators, the
great melting pot. Here players are judged only on the basis
of character and ability to execute — how much they have
to give and how much they are willing to give. Race, creed,
and background are not important. On the playfield and in the
sports arena some of the great lessons of life are practiced and
learned. Selfishness and personal glory are subordinated to
team effort and team glory. Here, under the white heat of

emotions, players learn that to control others they must first learn to control themselves. Good is not good enough. Continuous striving for perfection is the ultimate goal, and the dedicated player will settle for nothing less. To be complacent and self-satisfied has no place in athletic sports. A player or a team that is merely satisfied with winning would be satisfied to lose. Each game sets a new goal — a better performance than the preceding game. Nothing less than this will produce a winner, and winning is in the American tradition, not only in sports but in all areas of life.

PAUL E. BROWN, COACH OF THE CINCINNATI BENGALS

"He played the game" —
  What finer epitaph can stand?
Or who can earn a finer fame
  When Time at last has called his hand?
Regardless of the mocking roar,
  Regardless of the final score
To fight it out, raw blow for blow,
  Until your time has come to go
On out beyond all praise or blame,
  Beyond the twilight's purple glow,
Where Fate can write against your name
  This closing line for friend or foe:
"He played the game."

GRANTLAND RICE — BEYOND ALL THINGS

No soldier was ever made by the study of his manual, and no athlete was ever made by mere instruction. Both are made by hard, faithful drill and the perfection of necessary habits. Performance is all that counts when the game begins.

KNUTE ROCKNE

Defeat may serve as well as victory
　　To shake the soul and let the glory out.
When the great oak is straining at the wind,
　　The boughs drink in new beauty, and the trunk
Sends down a deeper root on the windward side.
　　Only the soul that knows the mighty grief
Can know the mighty rapture. Sorrows come
　　To stretch our spaces in the heart for joy.

EDWIN MARKHAM

　　Yield not thy neck
To fortune's yoke, but let thy dauntless mind
Still ride in triumph over all mischance.

WILLIAM SHAKESPEARE

Not in the clamor of the crowded street,
　　Not in the shouts and plaudits of the throng,
But in ourselves, are triumph and defeat.

HENRY WADSWORTH LONGFELLOW

I believe when you are in any contest you should work like
there is, to the very last minute, a chance to lose it.

DWIGHT D. EISENHOWER

TRUTH

Truth has no special time of its own.
Its hour is now — always.

ALBERT SCHWEITZER

Honesty of thought and speech and written word is a jewel, and they who curb prejudice and seek honorably to know and speak the truth are the only builders of a better life.

JOHN GALSWORTHY

Every great discovery I ever made, I gambled that the truth was there, and then I acted on it in faith that I could prove its existence.

ARTHUR COMPTON

Truth is within ourselves; it takes no rise
From outward things, whate'er you may believe.
There is an inmost center in us all,
Where truth abides in fullness: . . . perfect
Clear perception which is truth.

ROBERT BROWNING

I do not know how my work may seem to others, . . . but to myself I seem a child that wandering all day long upon the sea-shore gathers here a shell, there a pebble, colored by the wave, while the great ocean of truth, from sky to sky, stretches before him, boundless, unexplored.

SIR ISAAC NEWTON

Don't seek to live someone else's life; it's just not you . . . You have no right to put on a false face, to pretend what you are not, unless you want to rob others. Say to yourself: I am going to bring something new into this person's life, because he has never met anyone like me nor will he ever meet anyone like me, for in the mind of God, I am unique and irreplaceable.

ANONYMOUS

A man should never be ashamed to own he has been in the wrong, which is but saying, in other words, that he is wiser today than he was yesterday.

ALEXANDER POPE

To gild refined gold, to paint the lily,
To throw a perfume on the violet,
To smooth the ice, or add another hue
Unto the rainbow, or with taper-light
To seek the beauteous eye of heaven to garnish,
Is wasteful and ridiculous excess.

WILLIAM SHAKESPEARE

The doorstep to the temple of wisdom
is a knowledge of our own ignorance.

SPURGEON

Be not afraid of life. Believe that life *is* worth living, and your belief will help create the fact.

WILLIAM JAMES

Ethel Barrymore, Queen of the American theatre, asked the secret of her peaceful life, replied: "You must learn day by day, year by year to broaden your horizon. The more things you are interested in, the more you enjoy, the more things you are indignant about — the more you have left when anything happens. You must learn above all not to waste your soul and energy on little things . . . I suppose the greatest thing in the world is loving people and wanting to destroy the sin and not the sinner . . . And not to forget when life knocks you to your knees, that's the best position to pray. That's where I learned."

The greatest friend of Truth is Time, her greatest enemy is Prejudice, and her constant companion is Humility.

CHARLES CALEB COLTON

All truth is safe and nothing else is safe, but he who keeps back truth, or withholds it from men, from motives of expediency, is either a coward or a criminal.

MAX FULLER

They say best men are molded out of
    faults,
And, for the most, become much more
    the better
For being a little bad.

WILLIAM SHAKESPEARE

I say unto you: Cherish your doubts,
    For doubt is the handmaiden of truth.
Doubt is the servant of discovery;
    She is the key unto the door of knowledge.
Let no man fear for the truth, that doubt
    may consume her;
Only he that would shut out his doubts
    denieth the truth.

ROBERT WESTON — HONEST DOUBT

Nothing that was worthy of the past departs; no truth or goodness realized by man ever dies, or can die; but is all still here, and recognized or not, lives and works through endless changes.

THOMAS CARLYLE

Enjoy the blessings of the day ... and the evils bear patiently; for this day only is ours: we are dead to yesterday, and not born to tomorrow.

JEREMY TAYLOR

The submergence of self in the pursuit of an ideal, the readiness to spend one's self without measure, prodigally, almost ecstatically, for something apprehended as great and noble, spend one's self without knowing why — some of us like to believe that this is what religion means.

BENJAMIN CARDOZO

The great use of life is to spend for something that will outlast it.

WILLIAM JAMES

We do not please God any more by eating bitter aloes than by eating honey. A cloudy, foggy, rainy day is not more heavenly than a day of sunshine. A funeral march is not so much like the music of the angels as the songs of birds on a May morning. There is no more religion in the gaunt, naked forest in winter than in the laughing blossoms of spring, and the rich ripe fruits of autumn. It was not the pleasant things in the world that came from the Devil, and the dreary things that came from God.

R. W. DALE

Most people are some other people. Their thoughts are someone else's opinion, their lines a mimicry, their passions a quotation.

OSCAR WILDE

There is a tide in the affairs of men,
Which, taken at the flood, leads on to fortune;
Omitted, all the voyage of their life
Is bound in shadows and in miseries . . .
And we must take the current when it serves,
Or lose our venture.

WILLIAM SHAKESPEARE

Nothing left loose ever does anything creative. No horse gets anywhere until he is harnessed. No steam or gas ever drives anything until it is confined. No Niagara is ever turned into light and power until it is funneled. No life ever grows until it is focused, dedicated, disciplined.

ANONYMOUS

The tissue of the life to be
    We weave with colors all our own,
And in the field of Destiny
    We reap what we have sown.

JOHN GREENLEAF WHITTIER

Truth, be more precious to me than eyes of happy love; burn hotter in my throat than passion, and possess me like my pride; more sweet than freedom, more desired than joy, more sacred than the pleasing of a friend.

MAX EASTMAN

Every scientific truth goes through three stages. First, people say it conflicts with the Bible. Next, they say it has been discovered before. Lastly, they say they have always believed it.

LOUIS AGASSIZ — TRUTH

Neither a borrower, nor a lender be;
For loan oft loses both itself and friend,
And borrowing dulls the edge of husbandry.
This above all: to thine own self be true,
And it must follow, as the night the day,
Thou canst not then be false to any man.

WILLIAM SHAKESPEARE

It is better to light one small candle
than to curse the darkness.

CONFUCIUS

The quality of mercy is not strained,
It droppeth as the gentle rain from heaven
Upon the place beneath: it is twice blessed;
It blesseth him that gives and him that takes:
'Tis mightiest in the mightiest: it becomes
The throned monarch better than his crown;
His scepter shows the force of temporal power,
The attribute of awe and majesty,
Wherein doth sit the dread and fear of kings;
But mercy is above that sceptered sway,
It is enthroned in the heart of kings;
It is an attribute to God himself;
And earthly power doth then show like God's
When mercy seasons justice.

WILLIAM SHAKESPEARE

To be able under all circumstances to practice five things
constitutes virtue; these five are gravity, generosity of soul,
sincerity, earnestness, and kindness.

CONFUCIUS

Be thou the rainbow to the storms of life!
The evening beam that smiles the clouds away,
   And tints tomorrow with prophetic ray.

GEORGE GORDON, LORD BYRON

Knowledge and wisdom, far from being one, have ofttimes no
connection. Knowledge dwells in heads replete with thoughts
of other men; wisdom in minds attentive to their own.
Knowledge is proud that it knows so much; wisdom is humble
that it knows no more.

WILLIAM COWPER

Give me liberty to know, to utter, and to argue freely according
to conscience above all liberties . . . Though all the winds of
doctrine were let loose to play upon the earth, so Truth be in
the field, we do injuriously, by licensing and prohibiting,
to misdoubt her strength. Let her and Falsehood grapple; who
ever knew Truth put to the worse, in a free and open encounter?

JOHN MILTON

HAPPINESS

It is not easy to find happiness in ourselves,
and impossible to find it elsewhere.

AGNES REPPLIER

Happiness is not a reward; it is a consequence.

ROBERT G. INGERSOLL

Happiness is not in strength, or wealth, or power, or all three.
It lies in ourself, in true freedom, in the conquest of ignoble
fear, in perfect self-government, in power of contentment and
peace, and the even flow of life, even in poverty, exile, disease,
and the very Valley of the Shadow of Death.

EPICTETUS

We have no more right to consume happiness without
producing it than to consume wealth without producing it.

GEORGE BERNARD SHAW

The happiest heart that ever beat
    Was in some quiet breast
That found the common daylight sweet,
    And left to Heaven the rest.

JOHN VANCE CHENEY

Happiness is a butterfly which, when pursued, is always
beyond our grasp, but which, if you sit down quietly, may
alight on you. Happiness in the world comes incidentally.
Make it the object of pursuit and it leads to a wild-goose
chase and is never attained.

NATHANIEL HAWTHORNE

All the animals excepting man know that the principal
business of life is to enjoy it.

SAMUEL BUTLER

The ideals which have always shone before me and filled me
with the joy of living are goodness, beauty, and truth.

ALBERT EINSTEIN

Think of the hopes that lie before you
   Not of the waste that lies behind;
Think of the treasures you have gathered,
   Not the ones you failed to find;
Think of the service you may render,
   Not of serving self alone;
Think of the happiness of others,
   And in this you'll find your own.

ROBERT E. FARLEY

All who joy would win
   Must share it —
Happiness was born
   A twin.

GEORGE GORDON, LORD BYRON

Happiness is a by-product of an effort
to make someone else happy.

GRETTA PALMER

Happiness is the sense that one matters.
Happiness is an abiding enthusiasm.
Happiness is single-mindedness.
Happiness is whole-heartedness.
Happiness is a by-product.
Happiness is faith.

SAMUEL M. SHOEMAKER — ABIDING ENTHUSIASM

Happy the man, of mortals happiest he,
　Whose quiet mind from vain desires is free;
Whom neither hopes deceive, nor fears torment,
　But lives at peace, within himself content.

GEORGE GRANVILLE

Go not abroad for happiness. For see
　It is a flower that blooms at thy door.
Bring love and justice home, and then no more
　Thou'lt wonder in what dwelling joy may be.

MINOT J. SAVAGE

I went to purchase happiness —
　Exorbitant the price!
"None of your worldly treasure,"
　Said the merchant, "will suffice."

"But give yourself to others,
　And on the scales you'll weigh
A thousand fold in fervent joy
　You will receive today."

ANONYMOUS

There is that in me — I do not know what it is . . . but I know
　it is in me . . .
I do not know it — it is without a name — it is a word unsaid;
It is not in any dictionary, utterance, symbol.
Something it swings in more than the earth I swing on.
To it the creation is the friend whose embracing awakes me . . .
It is not chaos or death — it is form, union, plan, it is
　eternal life — it is happiness.

WALT WHITMAN

70

Take what God gives, O heart of mine,
  And build your house of happiness.
Perchance some have been given more;
  But many have been given less.
The treasure lying at thy feet,
  Whose value you but faintly guess,
Another builder looking on,
  Would barter heaven to possess.

B. Y. WILLIAMS

He is a wise man who does not grieve for the things which
he has not, but rejoices for those he has.

EPICTETUS

How soon a smile of God can change the world!
How we are made for happiness — how work
Grows play, adversity a winning fight!

ROBERT BROWNING

Happy the man, and happy he alone,
He who can call today his own;
He who, secure within, can say,
"Tomorrow, do thy worst, for I have lived
    today.
Be fair, or foul, or rain or shine,
The joys I have possessed, in spite of fate,
    are mine.
Not heaven itself upon the past has power;
But what has been, has been, and I have had
    my hour."

JOHN DRYDEN — HAPPY THE MAN

If I have faltered more or less
    In my great task of happiness,
If I have moved among my race
    And shown no glorious morning face,
If beams from happy eyes
    Have moved me not, if morning skies,
Books and my food, and summer rain
    Knocked on my sullen heart in vain: —
Lord, Thy most pointed pleasure take
    And stab my spirit broad awake.

ROBERT LOUIS STEVENSON — THE TASK OF HAPPINESS

An attitude so precious that it becomes a virtue is a gentle
and constant equality of temper. What an unutterable charm
does it give to the society of a man who possesses it! How
is it possible to avoid loving him whom we always find with
serenity on his brow, and a smile on his countenance!

EDWARD STANLEY

The happiness of life is made up of minute fractions — the
little soon forgotten charities of a kiss or smile, a kind look, a
heartfelt compliment, and the countless infinitesimals of
pleasurable and genial feeling.

SAMUEL TAYLOR COLERIDGE

FAITH

Whoso draws nigh to God one step
through doubtings dim,
God will advance a mile
in blazing light to him.

ANONYMOUS

Saint Francis came to preach. With smiles he met
The friendless, fed the poor, freed a trapped bird,
Led home a child. Although he spoke no word,
His text, God's love, the town did not forget.

ELIZABETH PATTON MOSS — SERMON WITHOUT WORDS

God has been so good to me;
    He has given me two hands
To pick His roses with —
    And two eyes — to see His rainbow —
Why should I murmur
    When they are aged and wrinkled
And He asks me to return them,
    For new ones perhaps?

JOHN SIMS — PERHAPS

Hope, like a gleaming taper's light,
    Adorns and cheers the way;
And still, as darker grows the night,
    Emits a brighter ray.

OLIVER GOLDSMITH

It cannot be that the earth is man's only abiding place. It cannot
be that our life is a mere bubble cast up by eternity to float a
moment on its waves and then sink into nothingness. Else why
is it that glorious aspirations which leap like angels from the
temple of our hearts are forever wandering unsatisfied? Why
is it that all the stars that hold festival around the midnight
throne are set above the grasp of our limited faculties, forever
mocking us with their unapproachable glory? And, finally, why
is it that bright forms of human beauty presented to our view
are taken from us, leaving the thousand streams of our affections
to flow back in Alpine torrents upon our hearts? There is a

realm where the rainbow never fades; where the stars will be spread out before us like islands that slumber in the ocean, and where the beautiful beings that now pass before us like shadows will stay in our presence forever.

GEORGE E. PRENTICE

The sun, with all its planets moving around it, can ripen the smallest bunch of grapes as if it had nothing else to do. Why then should I doubt His power?

GALILEO

O never a star
Was lost; here
We all aspire to heaven and there is heaven
Above us.
If I stoop
Into a dark tremendous sea of cloud,
It is but for a time; I press God's lamp
Close to my breast; its splendor soon or late
Will pierce the gloom. I shall emerge some day.

ROBERT BROWNING — O NEVER A STAR WAS LOST

No vision and you perish;
    No ideal, and you're lost;
Your heart must ever cherish
    Some faith at any cost.

Some hope, some dream to cling to,
    Some rainbow in the sky,
Some melody to sing to,
    Some service that is high.

HARRIET DU AUTERMONT — SOME FAITH AT ANY COST

Here upon earth eternity is won, —
The soul that seeks God holds immortal fire,
As tiny dew that trembles on a briar
Reflects the radiance of the rising sun.

THOMAS S. JONES, JR.

Faith is the substance of things hoped for, the
evidence of things not seen.

HEBREWS 11:1

There is no death; O, heavy heart
believe it!
Earth, sun and sky in golden chorus
shout it.
Cast sorrow in the fires of Spring,
nor grieve it:
Life is reborn in love; ah, can you
doubt it?

JOSEPH AUSLANDER

What delightful hosts are they —
Life and Love!
Lingeringly I turn away,
This late hour, yet glad enough
They have not withheld from me
Their high hospitality.
So, with face lit with delight
And all gratitude, I stay
Yet to press their hands and say,
"Thanks. — So fine a time! Good
night."

JAMES WHITCOMB RILEY — A PARTING GUEST

Science has sometimes been said to be opposed to faith and inconsistent with it. But all science, in fact, rests on a basis of faith, for it assumes the permanence and uniformity of natural laws — a thing that can never be demonstrated.

TYRONE EDWARDS

I know not where His islands lift
    Their fronded palms in air;
I only know I cannot drift
    Beyond His love and care.

JOHN GREENLEAF WHITTIER — FAITH

O, it is not for the rude breath of man to blow out the lamp of hope.

Instead, let us hold it high, a guide by day, a pillar of fire by night, to cheer each pilgrim on his way.

For have there not been times, O God, when we peered into the gloom, and the heavens were hung with black, and then when life was well-nigh gone, we saw a light.

It was the Star of Hope.

ELBERT HUBBARD

Prayer is a force as real as terrestrial gravity. As a physician, I have seen men, after all therapy had failed, lifted out of disease and melancholy by the serene effort of prayer. Only in prayer do we achieve that complete and harmonious assembly of body, mind and spirit which gives the frail human its unshakable strength.

DR. ALEXIS CARREL

O world, thou choosest not the better part;
It is not wisdom to be only wise,
And on the inward vision close the eyes,
But it is wisdom to believe the heart.
Columbus found a world, and had no chart,
Save one that faith deciphered in the skies;
To trust the soul's invincible surmise
Was all his science and his only art.
Our knowledge is a torch of smokey pine
That lights the pathway but one step ahead
Across the mystery and dread.
Bid, then, the tender light of faith to shine
By which alone the heart is led
Unto the thinking of the thought divine.

GEORGE SANTAYANA — O WORLD, THOU CHOOSEST
NOT THE BETTER PART

Lord, make me an instrument of your peace,
    Where there is hatred, let me sow love;
Where there is injury, pardon;
    Where there is doubt, faith;
Where there is despair, hope;
    Where there is darkness, light;
And where there is sadness, joy.

O Divine Master, grant that I may not
    Seek to be consoled as to console;
To be understood as to understand;
    To be loved as to love;
For it is in giving that we receive,
    It is in pardoning that we are pardoned,
And it is in dying that we are born to eternal life.

SAINT FRANCIS OF ASSISI — PRAYER FOR PEACE

So I go not knowing
—I would not, if I might—
I would rather walk in the dark with God
  Than go alone in the light;
I would rather walk with Him by faith
  Than walk alone by sight.

MARY GARDNER BRAINARD — FAITH AND SIGHT

Faith is the force of life.

COUNT LEO TOLSTOY

He is not dead, that friend: not dead,
But, in the path we mortals tread,
Gone some few, trifling steps ahead,
    and nearer to the end;
So that you, too, once past the bend,
Shall meet again, as face to face, this
    friend
You fancy dead.

ROBERT LOUIS STEVENSON

To an open house in the evening
  Home shall men come,
To an older place than Eden
  And a taller town than Rome.
To the end of the way of the wandering star,
  To the things that cannot be and are,
To the place where God was homeless,
  And all men are at home.

G. K. CHESTERTON

When on my days the evening shadows fall,
 I will go down to where a quiet river flows
Into a sea whence no man returns;
 And there embark for lands where life immortal grows.

THOMAS TIPLADY

Faith draws the poison from every grief, takes the sting
from every loss, and quenches the fire of every pain; and
only faith can do it.

JOSIAH GILBERT HOLLAND

                                        Whatsoever
The form of building or of creed professed,
The Cross, bold type of shame to homage turned,
Of any unfinished life that sways the world
Shall tower as sovereign emblem over all.

JAMES RUSSELL LOWELL

PATRIOTISM

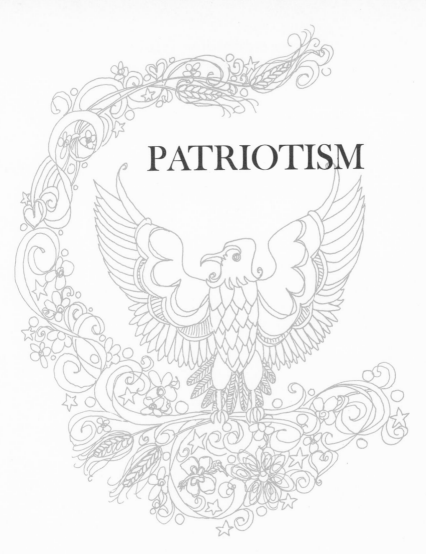

America! America!
  God shed his grace on thee
And crown thy good with brotherhood
  From sea to shining sea!

KATHARINE LEE BATES

I believe in the United States of America as a Government
of the people, by the people, for the people; whose just powers
are derived from the consent of the governed; a democracy
in a republic, a sovereign Nation of many sovereign States;
a perfect Union one and inseparable; established upon those
principles of freedom, equality, justice and humanity for
which American patriots sacrificed their lives and fortunes.
I therefore believe it is my duty to my country to love it, to
support its Constitution, to obey its laws, to respect its flag,
and to defend it against all enemies.

WILLIAM TYLER PAGE — THE AMERICAN'S CREED[1]

[1] *Adopted by the House of Representatives April 3, 1918*

God send us men with hearts ablaze
    All truth to love, all wrong to hate;
These are the patriots nations need,
    These are the bulwark of the state.

FREDERICK A. GILLMAN

Let our object be our country, our whole country, and nothing
but our country. And, by the blessing of God, may that
country itself become a vast and splendid monument, not of
oppression and terror, but of wisdom, of peace, and of liberty
upon which the world may gaze with admiration forever.

DANIEL WEBSTER

So it's home again, and home again,
    America for me,
My heart is turning home again, and
    there I long to be.

HENRY VAN DYKE

Let us ever remember that our interests are in concord and not in conflict, and that our true greatness rests on our victories of peace rather than those of war.

God grant that not only the love of liberty, but a thorough knowledge of the rights of man may pervade all nations of the earth so that a philosopher may set his foot anywhere on its surface and say, "This is my country."

BENJAMIN FRANKLIN

America First —
Not merely in matters material, but in things of the spirit.

Not merely in science, inventions, motors and skyscrapers, but in ideals, principles, character.

Not merely in the calm assertion of rights, but in the glad assumption of duties.

Not flaunting her strength as a giant, but bending in helpfulness over a sick and wounded world like a Good Samaritan.

Not in splendid isolation, but in courageous cooperation.

Not in pride, arrogance, and disdain of other races and peoples, but in sympathy, love, and understanding.

Not in treading again the old worn, bloody pathway which ends inevitably in chaos and disaster, but in blazing a new trail, along which, please God, other nations will follow, into the new Jerusalem where wars shall be no more.

Some day some nation must take that path — unless we lapse once again into utter barbarism — and that honor I covet for my beloved America.

And so, in the spirit and with these hopes, I say with all my heart and soul, "America First."

G. ASHTON OLDHAM — AMERICA FIRST

America lives in the heart of every man everywhere who wishes to find a region where he will be free to work out his destiny as he chooses.

WOODROW WILSON

Sometimes people call me an idealist. Well, that is the way I know I am an American.

WOODROW WILSON

So, then, to every man his chance — to every man, regardless of his birth, his shining, golden opportunity — to every man the right to live, to work, to be himself, and to become whatever thing his manhood and his vision can combine to make him — this, seeker, is the promise of America.

THOMAS WOLFE

It is to the United States that all free men must look for the light and the hope of the world. Unless we dedicate ourselves completely to this struggle, unless we combat hunger with food, fear with trust, suspicion with faith, fraud with justice — and threats with power — nations will surrender to the futility, the panic, on which wars are fed.

GENERAL OMAR BRADLEY

Behind all these men you have to do with, behind officers, and government, and people even, there is the country herself, your country, and . . . you belong to her as you belong to your own mother.

EDWARD EVERETT HALE

I think the true discovery of America is before us. I think the true fulfillment of our spirit, of our people, of our mighty and immortal land, is yet to come. I think the true discovery of democracy is before us. And I think that all these things are as certain as the morning . . . America is Here, is Now, and beckons us, and this glorious assurance is not only our living hope, but our dream to be accomplished.

THOMAS WOLFE

The outcome turns upon whether ours is a static nation resting on its laurels, holding fearfully to what we have, or a land which forever renews its youth by magnificent dreams and noble plans turned into great deeds.

DAVID E. LILIENTHAL

When an American says he loves his country, he means not only that he loves the New England hills, the prairies glistening in the sun, the wide and rising plains, the great mountains, and the sea. He means that he loves the inner air, an inner light in which freedom lives and in which a man can draw a breath of self-respect.

ADLAI STEVENSON

I have seen the glories of art and architecture and of river and mountain. I have seen the sun set on the Jungfrau and the moon rise over Mont Blanc. But the fairest vision on which these eyes ever rested was the flag of my country in a foreign port. Beautiful as a flower to those who love it, terrible as a meteor to those who hate it, it is the symbol of the power and the glory and the honor of millions of Americans.

GEORGE F. HOAR

For this truth must be clear before us; whatever America hopes to bring in the world must first come to pass in the heart of America.

DWIGHT D. EISENHOWER

Americanism is a question of principle, of purpose, of idealism, of character: it is not a matter of birthplace or creed, or line of descent.

ANONYMOUS

Everything is un-American that tends either to government by a plutocracy or a mob.

THEODORE ROOSEVELT

Well, I went in, and there, to be sure, the poor fellow lay in his berth, smiling pleasantly as he gave me his hand, but looking very frail. I could not help a glance round which showed me what a little shrine he had made of the box he was lying in. The stars and stripes were triced up above and around a picture of Washington, and he had painted a majestic eagle, with lightnings blazing from his beak and his foot just clasping the whole glove, which his wings overshadowed. The dear old boy saw my glance, and said, with a sad smile, 'Here, you see, I have a country!'

"... I am sure you know that there is not in this ship, that there is not in America — God bless her! — a more loyal man than I. There cannot be a man who loves the old flag as I do, or prays for it as I do, or hopes for it as I do." — *Philip Nolan*

EDWARD EVERETT HALE — THE MAN WITHOUT A COUNTRY

He loved his country as no other man has loved her, but no
man deserved less at her hands.

EPITAPH OF PHILIP NOLAN

Breathes there the man, with soul so
    dead,
Who never to himself hath said,
    This is my own, my native land!
Whose heart hath ne'er within him
    burn'd
As home his footsteps he hath turn'd
    From wandering on a foreign strand
If such there breathe, go, mark him
    well;
For him no Minstrel raptures swell.
High though his titles, proud his
    name,
Boundless his wealth as wish can
    claim;
Despite those titles, power, and pelf,
The wretch, concentered all in self,
Living, shall forfeit fair renown.
And, doubly dying, shall go down
To the vile dust, from whence he
    sprung,
Unwept, unhonor'd, and unsung.

SIR WALTER SCOTT

Acknowledgments

The editor and the publisher have made every effort to trace the ownership of all copyrighted material and to secure permission from copyright holders of such material. In the event of any question arising as to the use of any material the publisher and editor, while expressing regret for inadvertent error, will be pleased to make the necessary corrections in future printings. Thanks are due to the following authors, publishers, publications and agents for permission to use the material indicated.

ABINGDON PRESS, for selection from *Songs from the Slums* by Toyohiko Kagawa, copyright renewed 1963 by Lois J. Erickson.

A. S. BARNES & COMPANY, INC., for selection from "Beyond All Things" by Grantland Rice from *The Final Answer*.

THE BOBBS-MERRILL COMPANY, INC., for "A Parting Guest", from *The Biographical Edition* of *The Complete Works of James Whitcomb Riley*. Copyright 1913 by James Whitcomb Riley.

DODD, MEAD & COMPANY, INC., AND MCCLELLAND AND STEWART LIMITED, for "Autumn Song" and excerpt from "Vestigia," from *Bliss Carman's Poems* by Bliss Carman; for "I Meant To Do My Work Today," from *The Lonely Dancer* by Richard Le Gallienne, copyright 1913 by Dodd Mead & Compnay, renewed 1941; for excerpt from "The House of Christmas," from *The Collected Poems of G. K. Chesterton*, copyright 1932 by Dodd Mead & Company, Inc., renewed 1959 by Oliver Chesterton.

CONSTANCE GARLAND DOYLE AND ISABEL GARLAND LORD, for "Do You Fear The Wind?" by Hamlin Garland.

E. P. DUTTON & CO., INC., for two verses from "America The Beautiful" from *Poems* by Katherine Lee Bates.

BERNICE WILLIAMS FOLEY, for "Build Your House of Happiness" from *House of Happiness* by B. Y. Williams.

HARCOURT BRACE JOVANOVICH, INC., for "Courage" from *Last Flight* by Amelia Earhart, copyright 1937 by George Palmer Putnam; renewed 1965 by Mrs. George Palmer Putnam.

HARPER & ROW, PUBLISHERS, INC., for two excerpts from *You Can't Go Home Again* by Thomas Wolfe, copyright 1940; for one excerpt from "Steel" from *Cyclops' Eye* by Joseph Auslander, copyright 1926 by Harper & Row, Publishers, Inc., renewed 1954 by Joseph Auslander; for "Keep Some Green Memory Alive" from *Poems of Inspiration and Courage* by Grace Noll Crowell, copyright © 1965 by Grace Noll Crowell.